Smoke & Mirrors

Smoke & Mirrors

Donna Dallas

NY Books™

The New York Quarterly Foundation, Inc.
Beacon. New York

NYQ Books™ is an imprint of The New York Quarterly Foundation, Inc.

The New York Quarterly Foundation, Inc.
P. O. Box 470
Beacon, NY 12508

www.nyq.org

First Edition

Set in New Baskerville

Layout by Raymond P. Hammond

Cover Art and Design by Jake Dallas

Library of Congress Control Number: 2021935174

ISBN: 978-1-63045-080-9

S.P.B.

Along the winds
　　　My love
I heard you cry once
　　　as a soul
Before me
Before dawn
Before time and birth I passed you
　　　in a rush of plasma and light
I touched your core
Before you knew this life you knew
Me
Before your heart became a beat
　　　I loved you

CONTENTS

Smoke & Mirrors

In the Garden with the Devil

I
Don't look at me as if you know where I've been
you don't know jack about me
about my squalor
my decaying teeth
dirt under my fingernails
B.O. from not bathing
underpants too big they just slid down around my ankles
as I walked
through the garden......oh that garden dark and lush
in that secret place
my pit
where green ghouls laughed
at my entombed demise
die you little freaks!

II
dirty wretch I was
didn't know, did you?
sad fuck
twisted bones
torn inside from the birth sac
the golden fluid of me
dried up before I could scream out
say it
dirtbag
say it again
dirtbag
it swells in me
bursts when I bite the words

III
Tastes like over-ripened fruit
but you are my apple
and I, your Eve
behold I lay naked on the slab
the garden in me beckons you

come sit
laugh at what they called me
I'm sour at the thought of anyone's honesty
it's a scar hidden deep on a thigh
a covered wrist
concealing cuts that refuse to heal
blood seeps
into endless oceans of thought
and sad admittance that what they saw of me
and said back then
was entirely true

IV

If I was a dirty unkempt child
I can admit it now
as the bones of the past have milled
to mere man-dust in the garden of devils
in the garden of my sour apples
I am your seductress
your tainted Eve
I lay in waiting
under the blood moon
I've bedded Satan
allowed him to coil around my leg
to feast
come sit here at my throne
and cleanse my dirty feet
come

V

I will call you sire
love you eternally
I will sit on our eggs
warm them
hatch them
devour them

Over

Damn girl.
Look at you.
Who made venom
so thick
course through your blood?

The cold flow
of winter
is in you.
Blue blood, blue eyes,
dead heart.

Too many footprints
over your grave—rough hands
on your body.

Bastard girl
with icy hands
and cold lips.

No one loves you.

Stories

thank you Starbucks for my daily supply of English shortbread cookies thank you Lord for letting me go for not giving one fuck about honesty when you asked me how I was fairing now with all the medication when the week before I was screaming Mother Mary and bashing my fists into the wall over and over again to hell and back and I said I was fairing quite well feeling very rehabilitated lying like there was no tomorrow and eating one pack of those decadent shortbread miracles a day—and that was all—salvaging every fiber of straight-face to pull off normal for an hour or two so they would release me back into the world and my first stop off the crazy bus was our apartment where I waited outside for eight hours in the rain, stuffed myself into the doorway like a lumpy pillow and you stumbled up to me bloody shocked and I was fully aware you would call them up and make them take me right back to four walls of good and hefty padding where I could continue my soul searching but I ran ran ran for blocks for weeks for years and miles away I'm on the beach under your mother's maiden name with a flattering first name because Josephine was sooooo boring and I lick the salt from the glass and stare lovingly into Pedro's eyes as he says *yes mamacita yes my baby we good like this*...............

Skab

8th grade all the girls
have tits and they
wear lipstick. They
got their period. They
are constantly on the prowl
they ache for the boys.
I am straight, no curves, short hair
flat as a wall
ugly as a boy.
My period didn't come yet. I watch
the girls go head on for bases
with the boys.
They want the home run,
they want to fuck every boy they see.
The boy's eyes follow the curves of their
asses
follow to the crack between their legs
that they will open up and break holy bread
into.
I follow
wanting the boys to want me
to feel clumsy hands grip
my hips
but they are straight
they don't dance under a skirt
when I walk
cheeks don't peek out of short shorts
nipples are not erect like penis
blood not flowing here
from this canal
The cup is full but does not runneth
down the leg

Josie

but better days have come
        i wipe the sweat
        smell piss on my knuckles
        abortion residue
        drips down my leg
        dogs will piss on my grave

i'm coming into a moon
        full of pockmarks
        jealous old lantern
        lights my night
        lights my route
        down rockaway blvd
        into blue-black alleys
        where i give 20 dollar blowjobs

and in the morning i see Rico at the newsstand
        he gives me free smokes
        tells me to get some money to my kids
        who live with my mother
        or my sister
        maybe even a foster fondler
        who will rip little wombs open

crack
        i need my smack
        i need this pipe
        my lover
        my healer
        i smoke to God
        smoke to the moon
        and forget every crab corroding my body
        every pimp
        that yanked fistfulls of hair from my head
        forget the Siph
        the Gonorrhea
        the HIV

lead me not into temptation
       i have done only evil
       it fires my peace pipe
       i inhale over and over
       over and over

i wake up on the street corner
       in the back seat of a car
       in my lice-infested bed
       want more
       can't not want

Beastie

I wanted to write about those bitches
about how they followed me onto
the bus every day after school and spit
in my hair
about how they waited on my corner for me
to walk by and they hurled rocks at me
or chased me for blocks to cut me
to hurt

I was gonna put on paper how they crank-called me
just to call me names
Slut
Lesbian
Dyke
Cunt

I was gonna admit that......
yeah I stopped going to school
I stopped going outside altogether
and when they couldn't get at me
they would ring the bell and pleasantly call upon me
as if we were old friends
even study partners
but I wouldn't come out of my room

I was gonna say how it took a lifetime
to walk out the front door again and
I thought the passage was safe but they
no sooner found me and came at me
all of them

I wasn't sure if I should admit that I wished them
dead
every one of those ugly bitches
that bullied me because.....well.....
.......I never actually knew why
I knew only simple things back then
the boys liked me

the girls liked me
I liked me
then I never liked me—or anyone
again

after the first beating
when six girls jump on you and pummel
your face
you give up and pray to fade away into air

I was gonna say how much faster than me
I thought they were back then
much smarter
stronger
because they knew
I was a threat
and the only way to smite a threat
is to rub it out completely

Pureland

I took brandy from the sitter I placed it to my lips my tongue shrank
I kept to it I took the cigarette from your mouth
I took the needle pricked the vein I salved the sores
that festered between my toes and inside my thighs
I fought in the alleys and smoked the pipe I shared it
with whoever made it back I slept under the trestle I danced
ass cheeks out under a DJ screaming motherfucker
I prayed in a doorway escaping a rainstorm from
Mother Mary I crawled into a rancid bed that smelled—I smelled
I turned you on your side to vomit out of your mouth and not
choke to death I watched the stars with you sickened
with the HIV I confessed don't you know it
I told all until I was spent and reduced to a bug
I walked the bridge barefoot along the metal railing afraid
of nothing and if I fell off....if I did....
I watched thieves murder the innocent and ransack
their belongings I picked through took this and that
I swallowed all pride turned myself over to foster strangers
to heel me to study me because
only the strong survive in this......they want
to write about me what's there to say I've told it all
to that homeless clan who would listen in dead silence as I
coiled around them serpent-like with fascinating tales when
I ran through this city brimming with an insatiable thirst......

Ordinary Days

Some days
I forget that
I am nothing so
busy keeping
up with
the Joneses
that other person
of blind wind
zipping through the
streets fast and crazy
have to get
to work
attend the meetings
the PTA
grocery store
gas
all the places I need to go
then something happens
the dog pisses
on the couch
my kid is failing in school
I find
heroin needles hidden
under the mattress
of my bed
and my
dead
heart
is bleeding into
my pillow
I come back
to me
to the
nothing that I
originally was

The Burning Bush

They want to know what I think as I stare out the window
I'm thinking a rare filet mignon
a cheeseburger
I'm thinking.......when was the last time I dropped anything
off at the dry cleaners.......
I thought the garbage went out yesterday—I thought wrong
I thought
I pulled a soulmate out from that endless sea
of men
I thought your jeans looked a little tight
a few months ago   most recently I thought you
slimmed down almost back to perfection—almost back to that buff bod
we began
with
and I think to myself
why
why so perfect
now   years and years later
why am I more unkempt and you
are chiseled and razor   and yes we know   we always know
as I think along
I realize you created an inner circle of angst   that deadly ring of fire
in which our burdens from so
many yesterdays
burned through   small cinders
and sparks in the ash of here and now   and then I
think.......see what
we do when bitches are burned—it's the ugly
it's the raising of the center
of Dis   and there goes a cattle truck
I wonder if they know they are going to
die   the cows.................I try to think how do they kill them
the cows
I can't imagine what happens   and I notice the long road to our
home I don't even know the street names
anymore I just know the landscape   if I couldn't read I would know by
the
Flame bushes and the Ghost Maples

the Weeping Willow and
I think I know exactly where I am.......a young blonde woman jogs by
perhaps a
new neighbor I've never seen her before she's quite extraordinary and
I can't take my eyes off her   it's just a diversion
I think
just a way to stop
thinking   but thoughts are like air my
love.............breathe them in and in and never   enough
can't stop   can't function without.......
the thought
of you is
what kills me over and
over

Closed for Renovation

I try to pull the boy out from inside you
wedged up deep in your gut
squeezed under muscle
He peers out as
I twist and yank at
bits and pieces
of hair and some bone
attempt to whittle and mend
put him back together correctly
and place him gently in the cavity that held
your heart
such a mishap
what beset you that is so deep
we cannot
reach it
There is no recipe for the peace
that you long to wrap you
in a warm breeze heating the tips
of your eyelashes
You ooze out small weaknesses now
regrets seep through in the smoke
I try to grasp and
pull them into my chest
so your desires soak into me
then I can understand
and build a big cradle to rock you in
to cup the child
that was smothered
replaced with flecks of madness
we can't keep you any longer
you are slipping

Dumb as a Box...

Once as a child I caught the neighbor pick a booger from his nose and flick it
into the onion dip at our house party   I had always wondered
if people were really 'like' that
before I wondered I would ponder……stare into space and lie still as time
as Moses
as death
and think into worm holes through years what will I do when I wear grown-up
skin how will I ever get out of my head   how would I do all that shit
and fantastic wonder set in………

as if I could fly and wake God I grew in spurts
yearned for sky and some strange land beyond the four block radius
I tangled myself in the child
wrapping and cording myself into her hair
like spun gold
and opened from that cocoon a babe
my head formed a knot
I refused to pry myself from the thought of death
since it was blazed into
around
and inside me
I longed for a poltergeist   a night without end   yet I awoke again
aged
obsessing over things like
the color of our flatware
or the proper photo for our Christmas card

placed the wonder in the to-do draw and instead listened to mindless trivia
in my head
while others tasted of the wine and ate of the apple I fast-forwarded into
general malaise
and decided to open a book   a child's book of poems   she reads—she
lives and thought the world should know better than to close a book
I pried open a crevice in my head lonely as dust and age
felt wildly safe there in the dark
with the books, a shall….a limp that came with a cane
and still this all came in a heartbeat   while I was just lookin' up at the stars
in mere wonder……..

Breaking Bread

Scene 1
Halloween
1985
I, in costume as a space alien
You, as a pirate
Us, high as motherfuckers
Traipsing up 6th Ave
Raveling ourselves within the parade
Weaving in and out of painted bodies
Glittered lashes
Elvira in drag
20 Michael Jacksons
Dracula and his coffin
Stop only to snuff—me
Inject—you
Hours
The tin man / cowboy / green-wig girl
Limelight
I don't remember
Dawn came
At The Vault
I was pleasantly asked to pee on someone lurking in a pit
You were in the corner twitching
Sweat poured off you

Scene 2
Days later
Your ex knocked on the door
To leave your 1-year-old son
In your care
While she hit up a rehab
I was concerned about your Rottweiler
Around a baby
You left for a 4-day binge
I stole diapers
And used your cash
To get high
Not too high
Just enough
To carry on

With Lucifer
The Rottweiler
And your son
I realized the gold necklace
My godmother gave me was missing
You sold it to fund your binge
Rent was due
I never answered the door
Lucifer kept the landlord at bay

Scene 3
Halloween
1986
Me, your ex, your now 2-year-old son
All of us dressed as Elvis
Your ex
Now a lesbian
In love with me
And completely rehabbed
Wants to spend every waking minute with us
(But really me)
I am only on the drink
These days
You search for more places to shoot up
Running out of smooth skin
We watch in disgust as you
Inject under your ball sac
I slur
While you lean on the wall
For hours
Beer bottles litter the apartment
Ex is frustrated
With our addictions
Threatens to take your son
And move back to West Virginia
Whispers to me
I can't leave you with him
He will ruin you

This New Year's Eve

I list my faults. Lay them bare
like tarot cards across the table and
watch puffs of smoke explode above
me—I'm so bad.

I watch evaporating devils
bubble in my champagne.
They float up like unholy ghosts
into the air—bad girl all alone
this New Year's Eve.

And the neighbors are having a party.
Laughing and chitter-chatter trickles through
the cracks in the wood panels
The bubbles whisper forgiveness. I'm such
a tramp.

Angels are banging on the door.
If I let them in will I be blessed?

Will someone come and actually love
me tonight? One-night stands have
fallen flat.
Music travels through
the wall. Angels seep in under the door.
Relentless little things.

I tap the glass, look at
cigarette butts burning in the ashtray
all alone this New Year's Eve.

Phantoms

Bats flitter around me in the twilight under   our red
moon it's brilliant   I'm beautiful
still I don't want
to die / I wonder if the monsters on the other side of this
threshold refuse to seduce me because I'm too tainted............or too
easy?????

is this waiting game for your pleasure or my disarray...........??
I could try to pull something more out / stretch and wrap my tongue
around
my finger until I choke up words for   you

Am I moving too slowly or did I pop too many pills as the room vibrates
(Now there's a soft hum in my ear)
I watch you stare at that faint hint
of lonely I hover into / I can withstand a lot—monsters, demons /
vacuums of sad.......
but they didn't quite set me sober enough to envelope a parting

hold you're dripping heart in a chasm   take it out and fold it over
and over
like a good floured dough I want   I want to want but I
don't......morning arrives
birds chirp / angels buzz / perfect summer day ablaze yet
deep dunes open in the corners of my eyes where
tear ducts have gone dry as bone

Angels creep over the balcony as if I do not notice
they try desperately to undo these little sins...(which never
hurt anyone all that much.......)
a knock on the door / I just sit..............
mull your heart around
and around

Creation

Today
I'm a whore
as I stand before the mirror
examining this body
as erect as a penis.
My hand covers
the small patch of fur
like a veiny leaf straight from Eden.
Apple breasts for me—my gift
from God—as round as sin and
jetting out between marble shoulders.

I touch the hard thighs I have
wrapped around mens' torsos
to lock them into this torn womb
that has withstood time,
the stretching and ripping of
little imps and the weight of men
I try to forget
but it seems they have
made me into
what I am—right out
of a rib and I
am elastic flesh and
a bit of bone.

Stop blaming me
for being the seductress!!
I wear the key to Eden
as a slave trinket
around my wrist.
The snake has sided
with me and coils
around my left thigh.
I spit on Adam.
He's long gone under
mulch and earth.
I'm thin and ravenous
from running barefoot
through forests
and bedrooms.

Breaking God

3:46 a.m. I'm fighting demons
alone
I stare out into
longing   there's a want creeping up the side
of the building   slow and timeless
not placing it exactly my mind is foggy   there's a ball in my throat
alone   is a heavy net but here I am
after the party the after party the afterlife life after
alone
silly demons can't penetrate when the mind is loose
laugh madly at them
they cower in the dark   I fold them into the bedsheets
what's so silent that I am awake way before the alarm can shatter me
what's so dark I can pull it into me like a long drag
that last cigarette I never had
that last kiss I refused you
these are the moments when we grip ourselves so tightly we turn inside out
and yet it's still dark out there
while those wily bastards drain every drop
I'm bloodless
white and ghastly
crack open my cells and suck the golden yolk
I lay deflated over the moan of
what could have
now it's a whisper into murder's ear
not your death
but mine
only time will tell
when the break is

Sub-Divinity

There's that festering thing that
little regret / some little angst   can't put my finger on
it yet
its always with me some form
of Satan under
my collar pressed against my bone at the base of my neck   like a mole or a tag
when magnified one thousand times it's a
brutally ugly and distorted face I carry
cells that date back to the cross (did I throw stones??.....) to a night in the desert
when I caved and I can't shake the enormous
burden of paying
the piper I could end it you know...........why
keep going when it's all Satan-bound anyhow
I will end up there again it's like a calling
try to resurrect my blackened heart   reshape
it into a more compassionate heart—with honor and patience.......sounds
boring as Satan laughs but my torn
soul is tired
temptation feels hauntingly played   I think I
want a new skin—I want to peel back my forehead
reprogram a thousand years of whoring
go home and bake a pie   wring my sickness
into that pie like Stephen King's Thinner—let someone else eat it and
they in turn
take on these burdens while I stroll
away scot-free into the desert this
time an
angel

Woman

Take me to bed.
I remove
my
blonde wig
and now
you see
I am a
brunette.
Always
was.
There are
no more
secrets
between
us.

Man

All you want
is momma's
lap, soft breasts,
good cooked
meals when
you are hungry
and a slut in
the bedroom who
is not too
attractive because
you may lose
some sleep
wondering
if she's really
your girl and
not screwing all
your friends.

Sister

Somewhere she is fat & pregnant & chained to her ironing board
jelly-fat swishes around her buttocks / stretchmarks spanning the m
New Jersey creep along her belly & boulder breasts
her hair is filled with split ends & clumped together

like snakes on Medusa's head
She's waiting for husband #2 to come home with a six-pack
of Budweiser & maybe
some money for milk & cereal

She's got a roach crawling up the wall & #5 up her womb
heavy as a heifer
she is still smoking Newport's while #'s 3 & 4
piss on the couch.....

Dimwitted

There's a death in the air
floating up towards our window
of floor 37
I can smell it from the balcony
all hands on deck for it I salvage a tear
from my purse to show a little compassion
some mercy for fuck's sake every death
deserves a word or two
etched onto a gravestone
I sit waiting for it to rise up
as if it will grasp my sour heart
and I may breathe no more
but nothing happens
I exit unscathed the sun is shining
and I close death's door
your foot catches
we are full on writhing into a relapse
we drift into the same death
we miraculously escaped moments before

Love Story

This is where I say boo and you take a bow
on the threshold of martyrdom you thought
I was dying
half-rocked the tubes of life inserted
into every slit every hole plugged up emaciated
gray-eyed
head hung like a barbell
deaths door
you—avenger—cuckold
kept vigil over my bleeding womb
chant-chant
me back into eyeballs
back into a clit
single-handedly raise me
from the dead
I awake a mute
now what to do with me
un-dead
not her / she / the woman
anymore
scared you didn't I?
only warriors make a comeback like this
when you swallow mercury and it soaks into every cell
saturates every layer
then oozes through your pores
you become mercury
and you clutch onto me as the room floods
with water
we drift out
I worry you may catch a cold
as I burn full on into the sea

Lost in Visceral Bliss

They don't write good shit anymore   they can't pull the words out that choke your
heart into your throat   force you to take a seat   those words are dead
we invoke a plethora of meaningless verbatim   we miss it

we miss the mark of   honesty   because we are afraid to speak
   about the stuff that ticks in
us   I read somewhere the Mosuo women rule their village and Mosuo men
are 'at will employees'   they can stick around as
God fathers and uncles
not merely sperm donors   more than patriarchal monuments
   or parental consultants
I may sound like a feminist when I write this   but when I run
out at 6am in my village heels to catch a train   and leave my babies
at home with the nanny or the 'help' and their
Daddy
God father
Uncle
Sperm donor
Whatever the fuck
is on a truck whistling at twenty year olds   I wonder why I am not the ruler

Backlick Road

It's where you smell dog piss the minute you open the front door
where the dishes sit stacked up to heaven and Jesus knows I clear
them every fucking day
every sock
every important document
go missing
and later
they magically surface
when no longer needed
where I scream I'M IN THE FUCKING BATHROOM FOR CHRIST'S
SAKE at the top of my lungs
it's where there is a big beefy body in my bed and sometimes I touch
and wonder
who is this and how did he get here……….
it's where my mother screamed "don't buy this house you're out of
your mind!!!"
it's where every window…..every door and every floor
need to be replaced……………every lightbulb…………every
appliance
it's where I cry "where are we gonna get the money for this….!"
where kids come……..and stay
for days
where they eat it all
every crumb
where a beautiful child is chuckling
and giggles lift through all the rooms
where they keep coming in and out and I scream CLOSE THE
FUCKING DOOR
and they don't…………………
where coffee is served piping hot and perfect because finally
I was able to perfect   one thing
it's where lights are always
left on
doors always   open
mail constantly piled up
and there's that big warm body in the bed……breathing……he
touches my back
and it's quiet for one…….second

42

electric currents move through us
we are entranced   entwined with one another   as if we forgot
how good it really is
lost in hot breath...........skin
on skin
murmurs and muffled giggles   until the door flings open
and someone
strolls in
looking for the other sock.......

Queen of Bugs

At six years old I ran out of the house
every morning wearing little

white panties with three lines of white lace
my tiny nipples a smear of blush pink

barely visible at all while Mommy chatted
with the neighbors   they

stood around as I whipped by into the
garden—no not a garden at all but my

kingdom of bugs   I heard them whisper
about putting clothes on me.......that I was

too old to run around nearly nude but
I wanted to feel my skin on dirt and roll in the warm grass

dig holes in the ground with my big toe
my bugs were waiting   garden spiders plump and furry yellow

caterpillars and worms fat as sausages
I loved hearing the bees buzz around me   ants tickled

as they walked across my bare feet and
who knows what was tangled in my

long messy hair   their throne...........
princess of centipedes   grasshoppers   even

earwigs   big black beetles and the spider's
web, my altar of sacrifice—but only the bad bugs........

every day I served the large chocolate brown
spider hidden in the corner of the shed her

breakfast—black ants and horseflies caught
in the pool   a dying ladybug deserved

a proper burial and those chubby earthworms
were pall-bearers   and once a praying mantis

visited me among the tomato plants—me……..
a naked dirty thing in a pile of mud peering

into an anthill with bugs in my hair, between my toes,
in a jar under the bed, in my hand……..

Ingredients

Why write.....Why pour out the ingredients
that I own. Cannot speak—I could never
say it—the messy tangled yarn of words and

what would I say anyway? How could
you know I have died several times trying
to get it right, make us good, make you laugh.

I am bad for you? So is smog and secondhand
smoke and a good rare steak and what am I
to them if I am anything at all. People don't want

for others what they cannot have for themselves.
Why write when I could have told you,
or the mailman, that I believe I am reincarnated.

An old soul, a soul of souls—but I'm through
counting my lives since the end of the world is fast
on its way, an ugly vulture dragging half the

universe. So we must live life—really live it!
But what does that mean? I'm bored out of my skull
so I join the gym to get in shape and now

I'm bored with my own body. What I want
in the deep of a New York night is a good glass
of blood-red wine and the noises the cars make

when passing down my street.   People exist.
I forget this sometimes since I am quite occupied
searching for crow's feet around my eyes in

every mirror of every room I lay foot in.
I refuse to take all the blame for changing
your ways and probably nine other people's ways.

We bounce off one another and if I see white
today, maybe then I'll wear white tomorrow.
Why write about things like this—the stuff

I am made up of. How am I doing? I walk
on eggshells when I talk, stammer
and cough up blood for lack of words.

Diary of a Mad Woman

I want off this runway of
pretty dresses
high heels
make-up
nice-nice
Take me out of my head please
Naked I run on the grass
the cold dewy blades tickle my feet
I sit on a rock and stare at my boring pretty self
Later I open up the holes of my eyes and pour myself back in
walk on the beach and poach myself on a rock
Stare at the waves until I become one
Stare at you until you become me
and we swim in and out of each other
Again at the hands of fools I put the dress and heels back on
and wander aimlessly through the corridors of a building
I did not ask to be put in
You are on my back
your arms wrapped around my chest
and I carry you for dear life
While I walk over burning coals whispering softly
Ssssshhhhh
We'll be alright

She-Babe

I'm succumbing to prosthetic Gods
more and more. Fat women lay
in waiting for my jewels. I eat
their husbands. No remorse for
being the bitch.

I light candles for better stock.
I touch Wall Street through tarot cards
and send out smoke signals for a
guardian dollar to rock me to sleep.

(No more Valium!)

Momma still calls me cute and I want
her lap still. I smell her two thousand miles
away. But I smoke cigars and trade my slick
lips for gin and tonic.
I can't stand men but I want one to stay
and watch me cry once in a while.

Neverary

This is what I want love   come here......see me
for the monster I am   see my wiry hair / graying roots see
my crow's feet   love me still
tuck me into your nook......don't be afraid of the lunacy
I cannot control
I can only lie down
ask you to listen to this old tinker of a beating heart / centuries old
somehow still beating
you see my frumpled body and.....love me still
my heart still holds the fire
it grades up with age   because we never know what we are
doing
before we are thirty.......stay with me love
as we wait at some precipice
for all the wretched heartaches we still hold cradled in our boney
hands.....to pass

Heartache Misnomer

If there is a God
hidden
within these clouds
at 35,000 feet where everything is frozen
for 2 hours
on our private jet
I ask
does happiness come in a bottle
a pill
a sip
a drag
or is happiness inside
when I say inside I mean behind your bone
under your heart wrapped in your veins
like a rooted vine
happiness could be a weed
couldn't it?
because if you yank it
kill it
roll it over with a Mack truck
it will
inevitably
return
at some point
even at 35k
when the world is small
and I feel big
there is a hole
from roots pulled out
yet I siphon God
from a flute glass
ask him to save me
from
myself
I'm a hurter
they say
but only to my very own
core

51

Stars

Love, I dreamt you centuries before
I've seen your eyes, blue crystal drops on the leaves
Of trees thousands of feet away
I've touched you in the horizon
With my heart
Ablaze
For you
I felt you before
You were passed down to me
Under the starry eyes of God
I've given every breath
Every fiber
Rib and meat
To feed you to grow you
I am unclothed
Real
I bleed the truth for you
I scrawl a name into air
I push you out of my womb
I can do the pain
Again and again for you
Centuries born
To me
Dreamt you forever
Your code embedded in the stars
Through the passing of my breath
Onto your perfect face

Let Me Pull Out My Bag of Bones

I have lived a thousand years in this hull of a body
(waited to take you in)
to hold your cracked heart in my hand
mend it with putty and glue
Try to stick it back
(into the empty)
in your chest
fiddling with what goes where
(half-assed but meant with love)
Piece you together
(sort of.....)
then stumble around a muffled silence
weighing out if I can be good
(for once)
If I can hone in on a way
to show
strength
(for Christ's sake)
Once as a child we brought a puppy home from the pound and it
blundered
around haphazardly bumping into
and tripping over things
We realized later it was blind and would never survive
with the strong
(I am trying to survive)
That woman of strength
(I see her)
in a breath I take her into my lungs
force her to sit in my chest
(to woo you)
Later in the cold air of regret
I exhale her
(she's gone)
and blindness sets in

Lives (on Central Park West & 64th New Year's Eve circa 2012)

Look around you, love, and let's try to find them
The misery lovers?
No, the die-hard love hopefuls like me
They've never existed, baby, it's your wild imagination
Didn't the Murrans marry for love???
No, they married because they were both forty-four
And found no one
to actually
love
What about our neighbors, the Brennans?
They hate each other with a passion
She is fucking their tennis instructor
He's most definitely fucking their Swedish au pair
Well what about your parents—do they love?
Even secretly?
I've never seen them so much as smile at one another. No
there is no love there, hon
it's as empty as
your head
But my head is full of
the thought
of love—that it can be—can't it?
We're just playing it, love......we play our lives like a mad poker game
we win
we lose
we go on
let's drink some champagne
And you will smile and fondly touch my hand—is it love?
Jesus, honey, don't be so sad
love comes and goes in a wave
a climax
a look
a life

And Then There Were None

I hear the voices from the
womb in my head
whispers toil with me
the void is cold
ice-like
open and barren
skeptics and naysayers
step in to see
nothing comes out of it
but dust
Lying with charlatans and braggers
only to find fool's gold
keeping their trinkets on my wrist
I fiddle through dead space
and go it alone
Speaking in tongues
I drift with my travelling tomb
there is nothing in my belly
yet I feel a ball rounding ever so slightly
'Tis nothing
just the expanding
rhetoric seeping from the womb
that only exists in my head

Endurance
(sounds so excessive when used in a sentence to describe living)

I think I'm dying every day and every day I'm fine   I'm
frightened of the noises in the night / scared of my own shadow
—whatever—
I am highly educated if I stopped comparing myself to every other
woman I would
have the wherewithal to do something with those degrees rather
than stare at them while drinking a martini
fuck you
fuck me please
I hate you and I hate this roof / these shackles / these binding
terms
but I love you so—don't ever leave me!   I have separation anxiety
has never healed in me since
I was a child
and you / my caretaker / my protector   I deserve nothing / I am
nothing
yet I want everything—all of it
I take from this life   but what is the give back   am I even
supposed to give back?
where are our kids / our veins that we have cut and stitched
and cut and stitched again to make it right?
redefine a bloodline here and there when necessary / do what
we can to stay together when the priest mentioned two-thirds
of marriages end in divorce and for that pure moment we feel
"special"—in with the one-third—
later I want to strangle you
but it's all in a day's work   the tears—those crappy tears
......at least you can cry you say......

There's a Crack in Everything

I lean over the balcony to wrap my toes
in the Wisteria vine that creeps haphazardly around the railing
entwine my fingers in its velvet lavender petals.......watch balloons
lift off
from the forlorn wedding down below
slow birds in flight pale pink
and white they drift in a pack rising to the very balcony I stand
upon
linger for a second to sympathize with me as
I soak in shame
behind me sheets rumpled half on
the floor pillows strewn about
his body in a naked heap
guilt......sickening guilt.........
balloons float up like ghosts
pink and white
cigarettes snuffed out in a green glass ashtray
rot in the sun
I stand
wrapped in a white sheet
Cleopatra-like
wondering how I got here
from conception to.......deception
the womb is like a secret
tucked behind the pelvis to
warm
to hold
to escape into
and out of
dare to define a gaping hurt
as deep as earth
as sad and departing as pale pink and white balloons
light another
inhale deeper than a mothers' soft clean scent
exhale
stare straight into the sun
into God.....oblivion
secrets seep out

and over
a balcony
down a vine
into a budding matrimony
then drift back
sealed tightly in the womb

Self-Proclaimed Lunacy

Watch me
run—really run on the
wheel the
hamster wheel my legs are cut up bruised and
I'm gaunt maybe I'm dead—a running corpse—I
cannot see anymore I just hear the wheel
I complete the motions naturally since
there is nothing to see—blank   a big—nothing—me
and nothing go together hand in hand
we go together like the wheel under my bloody feet
my head oozes from the rotary vibrations
blood drips from my fingertips into my
water bowl I try to
stop but
it's an addiction how can I not yearn for
the wheel the nights slip
from me as I run and run and years
and tears and babies are boys are men and I'm still
on the wheel but now I am the wheel and the wheel
is me my bones have
replaced the metal   when I crack
into pieces and finally disintegrate I pray there
will still be an electric current left from
my original dynamic
core and you'll continue to hear it—the wheel..................
the motherfuckin' wheel

One Secret Thing

Live in this
they said
as they placed me
neatly onto the
pink rose-budded bedspread
in the room with white
and more white
so I would be well and
release festering thoughts
that wake me in the night
sweating thick to the point of oil
shaking to some madness of hot breath
on my neck
cold hands around me
But that was one night
one time
long ago in a life
not mine but the she before I
The she that was
lovely as a lily! they said
Death is a long haul when you wait for it
you slowly
very slowly
creep into it while no one pays attention
Shredding the malaise into parts to contain each day
it's the rotting from the inside out
whispers just under the skin
The Screwtape demon
forming a root in the rose-budded cell
with all the girlie stuff
The beckoning is cunning
over the edge of the bedspread
it waits
I somehow love it
yet I can't quite make out
what it is
Only death is certain

Afloat in the River of Styx

Put the cell phone down I'm lost in time   mad as a loon I want out
of traditional suits   out of perfectly made beds with satin sheets that wrap
my deadness
the world is slithering from me   I slink into the oblivion of yesterday
then ooze out to siphon Vicodin and Valium à la carte
roll a bill and swoop it across my white dusted mirror
the blur of fast coffee talks and Vive Clique   the evaporated doom
that falls every time I realize I am a small coward
faster each day / breathless / asphyxiated / constricted   and controlled
as time runs out
no savior as big as God   no male / no Voodoo doctor
can tackle this
white fence little house on the prairie / nice green grass decorated
with fuchsia flower beds
that little Chico comes out every week to preen
while I dice onions on the cutting board   and you breathe the wine
light up a Cohiba / listening to Bocelli / smiling like an imp / bigot / show-off
we are on candid camera
we are on 'we are fucked up' camera   and no one knows or sees
the degradation / decomposition / and extinction
of a happy wife   happy life gone
defunct

Melted

I'll try once more to be
buttery
sweet and soft
let it all go
start anew
try
deep breath
come undone
try
calm the nerves
seep into deep space
melt stars
I never get out
of my head enough
to realize
I am nothing
save the few bits of
blood and bone
I've left
squandered all the rest
on something
radical
I believed
as love
call it madness
I go again

Hell Hath No Fury....

When dreadful
whispers awaken
that fury within her
when she comes to understand
she has been deceived
that electric shock
that reboot
when scorned
devils cower
from her quake
she is coming
cunting
ravaging.....
be afraid

American Tears

We've danced this dance—you stop talking—I shut up into my own
later we'll have casual conversation in front of the kids
so they won't suspect   we are as screwed up
as everyone else
yet there was something brilliant—that thrived inside us
merged / made beautiful babies / entwined us for twenty-some-odd
years we had it
you and I   slow decomposition
happens with time………………..
here we are staring into space   thinking who can we sleep with
to get the other back—but really who wants us
now we are more or less middle-aged   we go on
because we have no one else
we can't quite break through to that old and gold love
we have tried babe—I know
last night I had a dream I was married to my former lover and in the end
he said he was just using me for sex
I woke up crushed and loved you madly for a minute now gone—
in the presence of each other
we only feel regret

Welcome to My Barren Womb Theater

I feel like a broke ass po' bitch from a trailer park in
the Everglades I feel like I did when I was ten and Lisa Sacristan picked
through my hair with a pen searching
for lice but it was just dirt and dandruff, Lisa, for the record………
I'm on a roll save me—save me from myself I ask
this sometimes when blood and guts ooze
out other times I'm dry as bone this time
1:04am in a town somewhere in the womb of the Gold Coast I hear
the world is falling apart one scorched woodchip at a time and I
can CNN or Google or Insta all the drama at any given moment yet
I'm so caught up in my own little world of
make believe the taxi drivers mouth dropped
open when he discovered I had no idea people died
in California or Oregon or where ever the fuck as
I'm too wrapped up in something called self-loathing and oh
yeah here is where I stop naturally but if I took it one step—just
another step over the edge of confession—you'd understand
I am a selfish NYC bitch with angst
that dates back to
dirty hair dirty feet and yeah they didn't show me how to wash how
to clean myself and when Lisa S picked through my hair I knew—I utterly
and completely knew how very imperfect—no no
that's not the right word—how
flawed
I really was and flaws root and flaws spread
like tumbleweeds through a desert and open up
into gaping balls of mental disarray yet I
pull it together so fucking perfect for 8-10
hours a day claw at myself on the train home
monsters in my head monsters under the bed…..still there
at night—the boogey man—I'm human I swear
I just want some quiet and enough mental focus to say
my last prayer for every creeping thing……

Modern Wives Club

They're on the Prozac and the Percs
I am with them in body
in yoga
in Starbucks
in Candee's Nail Salon
we shop couture
we do lunch
we stare into space
then ooze into our Mercedes
sexting gym boys
hoping to secure the future
fuck of a lifetime
I can pop a few of those
pink-coated bad boys
I wouldn't mind
the zone for a bit
but I'm missing stuff
so I prefer to keep it real
because one day soon
I will long for that raw
laying-myself-down-on-the-bathroom-floor-and-just-bawling-like-a-baby
emotion
Feel it
really feel it
my shrink says
I feel taller than a tree some days and
there are moments
when I prefer to roll myself under a moving bus
and let it all go to shit
but I wake up
clear-eyed
wildly aware
that I'm gonna die
no matter what
and someone
somewhere
in this house still needs me
even if it's just the dog

If There Is Nothing Left to Beg For...

The lover in my head knocks twice to enter / three times
to exit   shades my eyes while I sleep / whispers deadness
endlessly in my ears   I feel connected / through a vein   yet
I want him out
but he's so rooted I cannot detach   get the scissors / get the knife
surgery can be ecstasy...........................if cutting when aroused
I'm so blinded by thumbs   and so heavy from this body
ectoplasm oozes into me / somehow it's erotic   but my
lover is stagnant
it gets played—having him in my head
internally / externally
centuries born
into me he's got the foothold that Achilles
needed to win
I walk around / ask over and over to my
lover what do I say to this person / how do I
respond to that   how am I fairing
am I keeping up / am I smart enough????   can I have another please....

2019 Is Like This

I need a savior lord
knows   I need a slick
gin and tonic to slide smoothly
down my throat   vape cigarettes through a blue filtered pen
could trade places with sweet-at-home wives instead I
grind over and over but
all I really want is a cat
on my lap as I listen to the night
owl as I listen to the sharp cracks
in the fire when the logs pop and watch
the sparks fly out like shooting
stars   I am a mother / a workhorse / the underdog
I, the ample giver
caretaker
a getter
not a lover (…….well maybe sometimes)
I fold the sheets sloppily and I think
fuck it

Epic Wretch

I think I will stick around
I wanna see who my son brings home
who he will love I want to see
what my daughter's hair looks like
when she is sixteen and stunning
want to hear how the cardinal singing
outside my bedroom window sounds
to my ears at fifty
want to see if the world truly ends
and if my bag of bones will withstand

Mother Symposium

This
               B-O-D-Y
                              has housed other bodies......opened up for sad men
and closed up
for lack thereof
this body has multiplied to produce other bodies   has passed down
DNA that created amoebas, moved swimming molecular pools of though
into this
                        very body
where there are several bodies
including the body of Christ the body of
nobody
and everybody
this body has weathered great storms   the shifting of planets   it has witness
stars shooting into meteors
showering planets of no names
old names
has liquefied and slid down mountains into rivers
upstream into oceans
has dried up on sand and crystalized onto rock
                              this B-O-D-Y is old as fuck
it has given blood
a kidney
a vein here and there
an eye or two
this body has watered down the fires in Dis   has illuminated the dark
with phosphorescent light   has paved the ground with blood and bits
of bone to mark the path for Achilles, Attila, Spartacus, Julius, Genghis.
this body has laid itself down so you can walk over it and when you were
unable to walk
                        —this body carried you—
because this body is a singular
of a group
of a system
of bodies
of the body beautiful
a light catcher—a body liquid
and solid

and ever after
it encompasses sadness   endless tears are stored in all its' cavities
it sheds
it bleeds
it keeps
it shares
it turns
inside
out
for you
trail blazes earth to
               —please you—
so you can share in it
the body communion
take of it
and eat
take of it and walk through it
                into it
        give the body back when you are finished sucking it dry
it replenishes itself
rebuilds
buries itself in the mother celestial dust it was bore from
          Only to die……..
            —Only to die—

Death Collective

Line my coffin with
the butter-yellow Austrians
from our beach cottage
bedroom with
that cathedral ceiling we loved
to stare up into
forever
Pull some Venetian prisms
off the hundred-year-old
chandelier that flickered sun-holes
onto us from the window and make
earrings out of them for me please
You can lay me into a mahogany casket
with my black Chanel
the one we bought
on Place Vendome
in the midst of a rain so heavy
it was God upon us
Slip my Louboutins on feet
hard as stone
bend the toes so my arch is angled to the shape
of that divine heel
don't put a ton of makeup on me
I don't want to look garish
at the wake and scare away
the handful of viewers goggling
over my long and broken body
Burn me after
light me up
howl at the fire
I smolder and catapult up the shaft
in a whirlwind of smoke and ash
Finger through the soot
to find a nail
or a piece of a tooth
perhaps a bit of hair
save it
love it
it was me you bastard

Everyone Wants a Piece of Donna

stop with the *Donna do ya wanna*
stop with the song *Oh Donna*
stop pulling my sleeve
kids on the tit
IRS up my ass
slave to the white collar
industry whore
only workaholics can play this game
job after job
to feed you
educate you
globalize you
a cultural necklace of continents
baubles and pearls
only to end up in a box
later grandchildren will roll them around in sticky fingers
ooohhhing
and aahhhing at the mysteries
that we discovered
on the Amex platinum
places where
red moons fused into
glorious pink sunrises
panoramic landscapes that could
stop the heart
when that heart stops
when Donna ceases to exist
when Donna is *OOO*
Out Of Office you fools
Donna will chisel her initials
into the limestone
of the cavern
she winds down into
like Jesus
laid to rest in Jerusalem
they will push the rock out from the cave
pick at my body
place a flower on my lips

coins over my eyes for what I was worth
pull a tooth
a cutting of hair
body souvenirs
the keepsakes
from D.A.D.
slide the rock back
and place a sign that reads
D.N.D.

Acknowledgments

In the Garden with the Devil	—	*Red Fez*
Over	—	*Vending Machine Press*
Stories	—	*Red Fez*
Skab	—	*The Opiate*
Josie	—	*Visceral Uterus*
Beastie	—	*Anti-Heroin Chic*
Pureland	—	*The Opiate*
Ordinary Days	—	*The Opiate*
The Burning Bush	—	*Anti-Heroin Chic*
Closed for Renovation	—	*The Opiate*
Dumb as a Box...	—	*Red Fez*
Breaking Bread	—	*The Opiate*
This New Year's Eve	—	*Public Pool*
Phantoms	—	*Velvet Giant*
Creation	—	*Vending Machine Press*
Breaking God	—	*Quail Bell Magazine*
Sub-Divinity	—	*The Opiate*
Man	—	*Punklit Press*
Sister	—	*The Opiate*
Dimwitted	—	*Thirteen Myna Birds*
Love Story	—	*Thirteen Myna Birds*
Lost in Visceral Bliss	—	*Dum Dum Zine*
Backlick Road	—	*Red Fez*
Queen of Bugs	—	*Oddball Magazine*
Ingredients	—	*Drunk Monkeys*
Diary of a Mad Woman	—	*Quail Bell Magazine*
She-Babe	—	*Picaroon Poetry*
Neverary	—	*Foliate Oak Literary Magazine*
Heartache Misnomer	—	*Burning House*
Stars	—	*Foliate Oak Literary Magazine*
Let Me Pull Out My Bag of Bones	—	*Vending Machine Press*
Lives (on Central Park West & 64th New Year's Eve circa 2012)	—	*Misfit Magazine*
And Then There Were None	—	*Horror Zine*
Endurance (sounds so excessive when used in a sentence to describe living)	—	*Visceral Uterus*

www.ingramcontent.com/pod-product-compliance
Lightning Source LLC
Chambersburg PA
CBHW022016080426
42733CB00007B/622